To: Sandie
Merry Christmas
and a very happy 2018
Love you.
Beverley

# What Birds Teach Us

Published by Willow Creek Press, Inc.
P.O. Box 147, Minocqua, Wisconsin 54548

Photo Credits:

p4 © Franz Christoph Robiller/imageBROKER/age fotostock; p7 © Henny Brandsma/Buiten-beeld/Minden Pictures;
p8 © M. Delpho/Arco/age fotostock; p11 © Thorsten Milse/age fotostock; p12 © H. Jegen/Arco/age fotostock;
p15 © Donald M. Jones/Minden Pictures; p16 © Donald M. Jones/Minden Pictures;
p19 © Nobuaki Hirano/Nature Production/Minden Pictures; p20 © Corbis/age fotostock; p23 © Sean Crane/Minden Pictures;
© Andrew Parkinson/NPL/Minden Pictures; p26 © M Woike/Blickwinkel/age fotostock; p29 © John Eveson/FLPA/Minden Pictures;
p30 © PhotoStock-Israel/age fotostock; p33 © Andrew Bailey/FLPA/Minden Pictures; p34 © Tui De Roy/Minden Pictures;
p37 © Wil Meinderts/Buiten-beeld/Minden Pictures; p38 © Alan Murphy/BIA/Minden Pictures;
p41 © Stephen Belcher/Minden Pictures; p42 © Jan Uilhoom/Buiten-beeld/Minden Pictures; p45 © Classic Stock/Masterfile;
p46 © gero b/Zoonar GmbH/age fotostock; p49 © Michael & Patricia Fogden/Minden Pictures;
p50 © Yva Momatiuk & John Eastcott/Minden Pictures; p52 © Otto Plantema/Buiten-beeld/Minden Pictures;
p55 © Tim Fitzharris/Minden Pictures; p56 © Heini Wehrle/Minden Pictures;
p59 © Henny van Egdom/Buiten-beeld/Minden Pictures; p60 © Suzi Eszterhas/Minden Pictures; p63 © Tui De Roy/Minden Pictures;
p64 © Jan Wegener/BIA/Minden Pictures; p67 © Paul Hobson/NPL/Minden Pictures; p68 © Roger Tidman/FLPA/Minden Pictures;
p71 © Ingo Arndt/Minden Pictures; p72 © Jiri Slama/BIA/Minden Pictures; p74 © Suzi Eszterhas/Minden Pictures;
p77 © Jan Wegener/BIA/Minden Pictures; p78 © Graeme Guy/BIA/Minden Pictures; p81 © Bill Baston/FLPA/Minden Pictures;
p82 © Konrad Wothe/Minden Pictures; p85 © Sergey Gorshkov/Minden Pictures; p86 © Malcolm Schuyl/FLPA/age fotostock;
p88 © Ernst Dirksen/Buiten-beeld/Minden Pictures; p91 © Michael Eudenbach/Masterfile;
p92 © Andrew Parkinson/2020VISION/NPL/Minden Pictures; p95 © Matthias Breiter/Minden Pictures;
p96 © S & D & K Maslow/FLPA/age fotostock

Design: Donnie Rubo
Printed in China

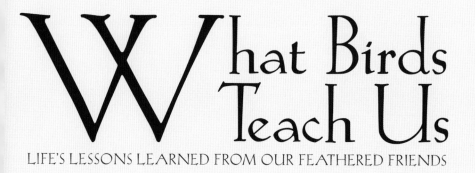

# What Birds Teach Us

## LIFE'S LESSONS LEARNED FROM OUR FEATHERED FRIENDS

*Bonnie Louise Kuchler*

**WILLOW CREEK PRESS®**

# HATCHING & FLEDGING

You cannot go on indefinitely
being just an ordinary, decent egg.
We must be hatched or go bad.

—C. S. Lewis (1898-1963)
*British novelist*

When you first break out of your shell,
it's normal to feel vulnerable—
to feel anything but confident.

Northern Lapwing parent and chicks

Great-crested Grebe

It's humbling to ask for help.
Do it anyway.
You need all the nourishment and knowledge
you can get out there.

Nothing is more important than family.

*Emperor Penguin parent and chick*

Build up your wing muscles.

When you outgrow that once-cozy nest,

you'll be ready:

You'll have the power to fly.

Don't let fear hold you back.
Let it drive you toward your dreams.

Long-eared Owlet

# LEARNING TO FLY

Sometimes you just gotta be
drop-kicked out of the nest.

—*Robert Downey, Jr.*
*American actor*

To fly, you must let go of solid ground.

If you can't get off the ground,
your wing-to-weight ratio may be low.
Perhaps you need bigger wings
or less baggage.

If it's too heavy for you to carry,
you need to let it go.

Once airborne,
you're at the mercy of a capricious host.
The wind will shift,
and you must adapt.
Learn to adjust your flaps.

# SURVIVING

The shaft of the arrow had been feathered with
one of the eagles own plumes.
We often give our enemies the means
of our own destruction.

—*Aesop*

Don't go flying through doorways head-first,
no matter how inviting they look.

Focus your sights.

You can't hit a target if you can't see it.

The one who works hard
will take home the worms.

Masked Weaver

If you want to get paid, finish the job—
tie up all the loose ends.
Scarce are the rewards for a job half done.

*Mother Nature* is a bit of a misnomer.
Nature doesn't reward, punish, or coddle.
And nature will never protect you
from yourself.

# MIGRATING

As with the migrant birds,
so surely with us, there is a voice within...
that tells us so certainly
when to go forth into the unknown.

—*Elisabeth Kübler-Ross (1926-2004)*
*Swiss-American psychiatrist and author*

Be willing to lose sight of the shore.

*Black-browed Albatross*

Tomorrow is that unseen country
where dreams live and die
and hope learns to fly.

Trust your instincts.
When a destination calls you,
your course will stay true.

*Geese*

*Andean Condor*

Steer clear of downdrafts.
If you want to soar,
seek out warm, uplifting currents.

If you flap too much
you'll wear yourself out,
unless, of course, you're a hummingbird.
Which you're not.

*Sandhill Cranes*

Whenever possible,
take the scenic route.

# FEATHERED FRIENDS
# & TALONED FOES

It's not where you go,

it's who you travel with.

—*Charles M. Schulz (1922-2000)*
*American cartoonist*

Sharing simple pleasures with friends
sweetens any journey.

Be suspect of any companion
who does not give and take.
A friend, even in the taking,
hopes that some pleasure is
gained in the giving.

Just because you won't eat the hawk,
doesn't mean the hawk won't eat you.

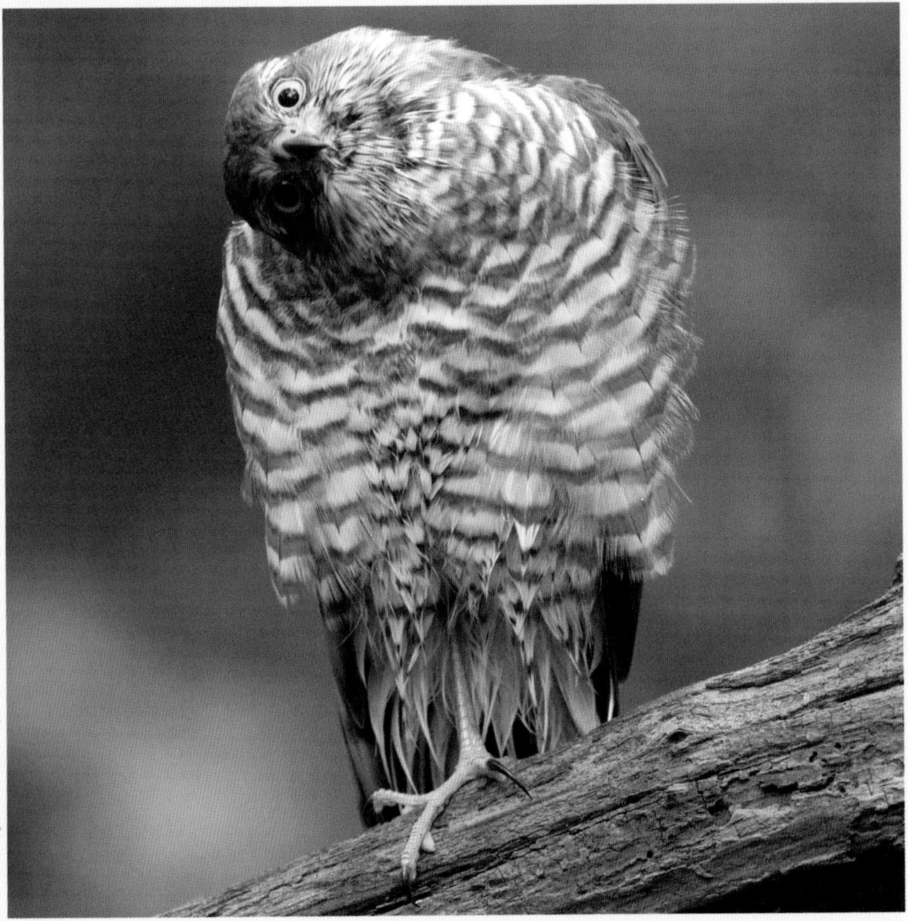

*Eurasian Sparrowhawk juvenile*

*Hyacinth Macaws*

You can learn a lot about someone
over dinner.

Watch as much as you listen.
More than half of what we say
isn't out loud.

# FINDING A MATE

If it is your time,
love will track you down
like a cruise missile.

—*Lynda Barry*
*American cartoonist and writer*

You can attract the attention of a
future mate in many ways—
once you get past the learning curve.

European Bee-eaters

Display confidence,
and show off your best features.

Whatever your future mate wants most,
show that you can make it happen.
With flair!

A gift doesn't need to be big
to be meaningful.

# FULL NEST, EMPTY NEST

There are only two lasting bequests
we can give our children.
One of these is roots,
the other, wings.

*—Hodding Carter (1907-1972)*
*American journalist and author*

If you have the urge to nest,
both of you must be eager and ready for
a tiny nestling with enormous needs.

*Coppersmith Barbet parent and chick*

Filling hungry mouths is
entirely exhausting and deeply satisfying.

By far the sweetest agony comes
when you teach them to fly.
And they do.

*Barn Swallow parent and juvenile*

Grey Heron

Life isn't over when the kids leave home.
It's time to rediscover you,
to reconnect with your own life.

If it's any comfort,
once they're on their own
they'll still call when they
need your help.

*African Fish Eagles*

*Bewick's Swan adult and juvenile*

Don't fret that a childhood has ended.
Think of it as your promotion—
from teacher to friend.

Bearded Tit

# THRIVING

All the art of living lies in a fine mingling
of letting go and holding on.

*—Havelock Ellis (1859-1939)*
*English essayist and physician*

Nature speaks,
but you must be very quiet
to hear her.

*Coot*

Whatever you're seeking,
look deeper than the surface.

No matter how high, how far,
or how long you fly,
you still need landing gear.
For sooner or later,
every flight must come to an end.

*Cedar Waxwing*

It's not the branch you need to believe in.

It's your wings.